PEGASUS ENCYCLOPEDIA LIBRARY

Continents
NORTH AMERICA

Edited by: Pallabi B. Tomar, Hitesh Iplani
Managing editor: Tapasi De
Designed by: Vijesh Chahal, Anil Kumar, Rohit Kumar
Illustrated by: Suman S. Roy, Tanoy Choudhury
Colouring done by: Vinay Kumar, Kiran Kumari & Pradeep Kumar

NORTH AMERICA

CONTENTS

Introduction 3

List of countries 7

Geography 9

Natural resources 13

Climate 14

History 15

Religion 17

Festivals 18

Famous places 22

Famous people 28

Test Your Memory 31

Index 32

Introduction

North America is the third-largest continent on Earth after Asia and Africa. It covers about 4.8 per cent of the Earth's surface. Most of the continent lies in the northern hemisphere between the Arctic Circle and the Tropic of Cancer.

It is almost completely surrounded by bodies of water, including the Pacific Ocean, the Bering Strait, the Arctic Ocean, the Atlantic Ocean and the Caribbean Sea and Gulf of Mexico. The only strip of land connecting North America to South America is the narrow Isthmus of Panama.

Three major countries, which occupy most of the land space of the continent, are Canada, Mexico and the United States. Central America and the Caribbean are usually considered to be a part of North America. Though geographically Greenland is a part of the continent of North America, politically it is a part of the European Union.

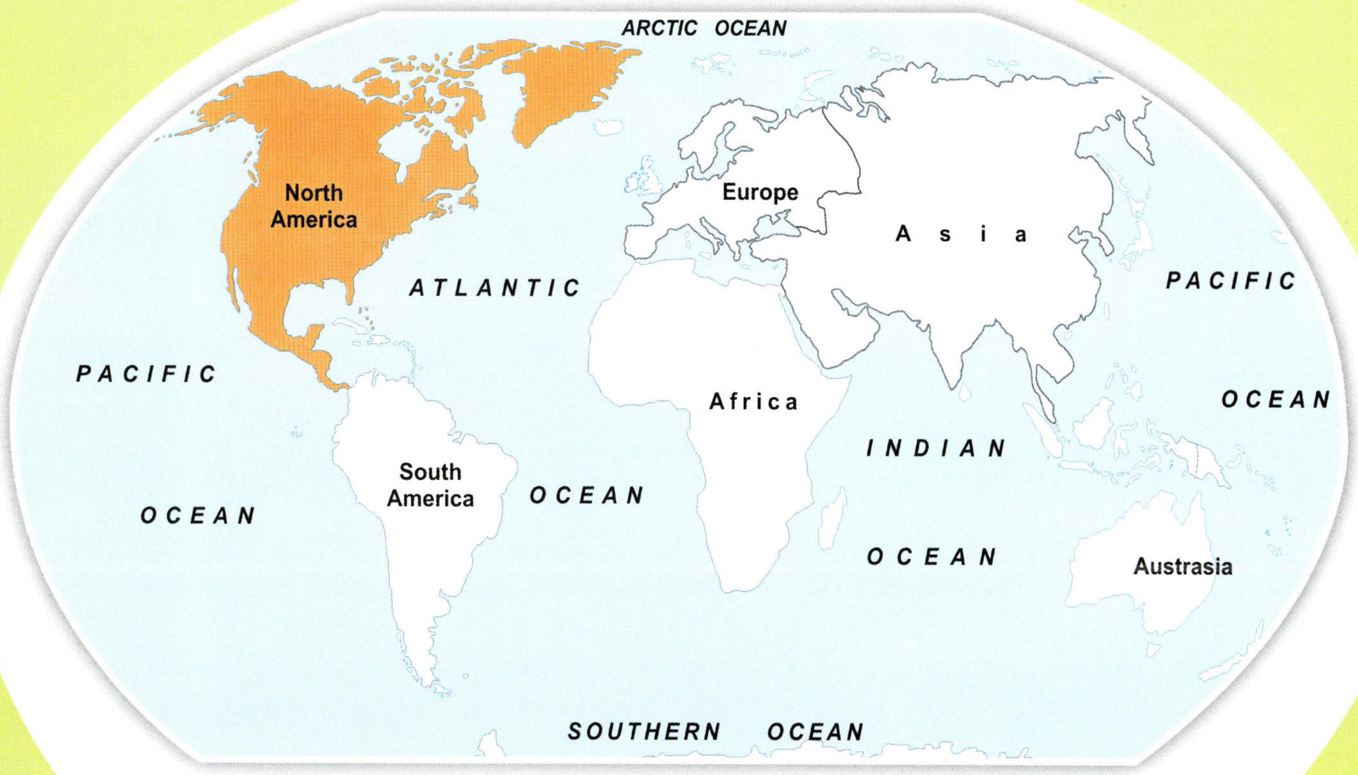

NORTH AMERICA

North America is bordered on the north by the Arctic Ocean, on the east by the North Atlantic Ocean, on the south by the Caribbean Sea and on the west by the North Pacific Ocean. The Panama Canal and the continent of South America lie to the south of North America

People

North America is inhabited by three major groups. The largest group is that of the descendants of European colonists and immigrants. Most of the population in the United States, Canada and some Central American and West Indian areas is made up of this group. Though the descendants of African slaves are found in the United States, they form a majority population group only in Belize and some West Indian areas, particularly Haiti.

> **The name America comes from the name of an early explorer of the region, Amerigo Vespucci, who was the first European to suggest that the Americas were not a part of Asia as Christopher Columbus had suggested; instead they were part of an undiscovered New World.**

Introduction

The descendants of North America's native inhabitants, the Indians and Eskimos are minority groups in Canada and the United States. Parts mostly inhabited by the Indians are Mexico and Central America. People of mixed ancestry, mostly European-Indian and European-African origin also inhabit Mexico, Central America and the West Indies.

Eskimos

The United States, Canada and the other English-speaking nations of the Americas (Belize, Guyana, and the Anglophone Caribbean) are sometimes grouped under the term **Anglo-America**, while the remaining nations of North and South America are grouped under the term **Latin America**.

The term Northern America is used to refer to Canada and the U.S. together (plus Greenland and Bermuda), while Central America is a part of the mainland south of the United States. The West Indies generally includes all islands in the Caribbean Sea. In this respect, Latin America generally includes Central America and South America and sometimes, the West Indies. The term Middle America is sometimes used to refer to Mexico, Central America and the Caribbean collectively.

NORTH AMERICA

North America at a glance

Area	24,212,000 km2
Maximum distances (Mainland)	
North-South	7, 200 km
East-West	6, 400 km
Maximum distances (including islands)	
North-South	8,900 km
East-West	8,900 km
Coastline	300,000 km
Highest point	McKinley in Alaska (6,194 m above sea level)
Lowest point	Death Valley (86 m below sea level)
Number of independent countries	23

Death Valley

Languages

Various languages, both European and native, are spoken in America. English is primarily spoken in Canada, USA and Belize. Spanish is the chief language of the countries of Latin America and a minority in the USA. French is spoken by about 25 per cent of the population of Canada and by people of the French possession of St Pierre and Miquelon. The native non-European minorities including the Inuit of Arctic Canada, the Aleuts of Alaska, North American Indians and the Maya of Central America, have their own languages and dialects.

List of countries

	Flag	English name	Capital	Currency	Language
1.		Antigua and Barbuda	St. John's	East Caribbean dollar	English
2.		Bahamas	Nassau	Bahamian dollar	English
3.		Barbados	Bridgetown	Barbadian dollar	English
4.		Belize	Belmopan	Belize dollar	English, Spanish
5.		Canada	Ottawa	Canadian dollar	English, French
6.		Costa Rica	San José	Costa Rican colón	Spanish
7.		Cuba	Havana	Cuban peso, Chavito	Spanish
8.		Dominica	Roseau	East Caribbean dollar	English
9.		Dominican Republic	Santo Domingo	Dominican Peso	Spanish
10.		El Salvador	San Salvador	United States dollar	Spanish
11.		Grenada	St. George's	East Caribbean dollar	English
12.		Guatemala	Guatemala City	Guatemalan quetzal	Spanish

NORTH AMERICA

13.		Haiti	Port-au-Prince	Haitian gourde	French
14.		Honduras	Tegucigalpa	Honduran lempira	Spanish
15.		Jamaica	Kingston	Jamaican dollar	English
16.		Mexico	Mexico City	Mexican Peso	Spanish
17.		Nicaragua	Managua	Nicaraguan córdoba	Spanish
18.		Panama	Panama City	Panamanian balboa, United States dollar	Spanish
19.		Saint Kitts and Nevis	Basseterre	East Caribbean dollar	English
20.		Saint Lucia	Castries	East Caribbean Dollar	English
21.		Saint Vincent and the Grenadines	Kingstown	East Caribbean dollar	English
22.		Trinidad and Tobago	Port of Spain	Trinidad and Tobago dollar	English
23.		United States	Washington, D.C.	United States dollar	English

Since 1931, Rugby, North Dakota, has officially been recognized as the geographical centre of North America. A 4.5 m stone obelisk (a tall, slender, four-sided stone pillar tapering at the top) marks the spot.

Geography

Northernmost point	Boothia Peninsula in the Canadian Arctic region
Southernmost point	Punta Mariato on the Isthmus of Panama
Westernmost point	Cape Prince of Wales, Alaska
Easternmost point	Cape St Charles on the coast of Labrador, Canada

North America can be divided into six major landform divisions namely the **Coastal Plains**, the **Canadian Shield**, the **Interior Plains**, the **Appalachian Highlands**, the **North American Cordillera** and the **Antillean System**.

The **Coastal Plains** extend along the eastern coast from Mexico to Cape Cod. It continues offshore, emerging southeast of Florida to form the Bahamas Islands. The mainland portion of the Coastal Plain is narrow in the northeast but reaches a width of more than 640 km in the lower Mississippi River Valley. The low, generally flat plain rises slightly as it extends inland, where it is bordered by higher land for most of its length.

The **Canadian Shield** or the **Laurentian Plateau** covers Greenland and much of central and northern Canada and extends into the United States in the Superior Uplands and the Adirondack Mountains. It is composed of hard crystalline rock scoured by glaciers that left hundreds of lakes. The plateau is about 300 m above sea level, decreasing slightly westward and southward.

Rocky Mountains

The **Interior Plains** region is a vast, relatively level area occupying a large part of the continent's interior. It lies between the Appalachian Highlands, the Canadian Shield, and the Rocky Mountains and merges with the Coastal Plain in the south.

In the east are the **Central Lowlands**, which are about 180 m above sea level. The Great Plains in the west is relatively flat grassland ascending slowly to a maximum of 1,800 m at its western edge, the Rocky Mountains. Two small highland areas are often included within the Interior Plains—the Black Hills of South Dakota and the Central Uplands.

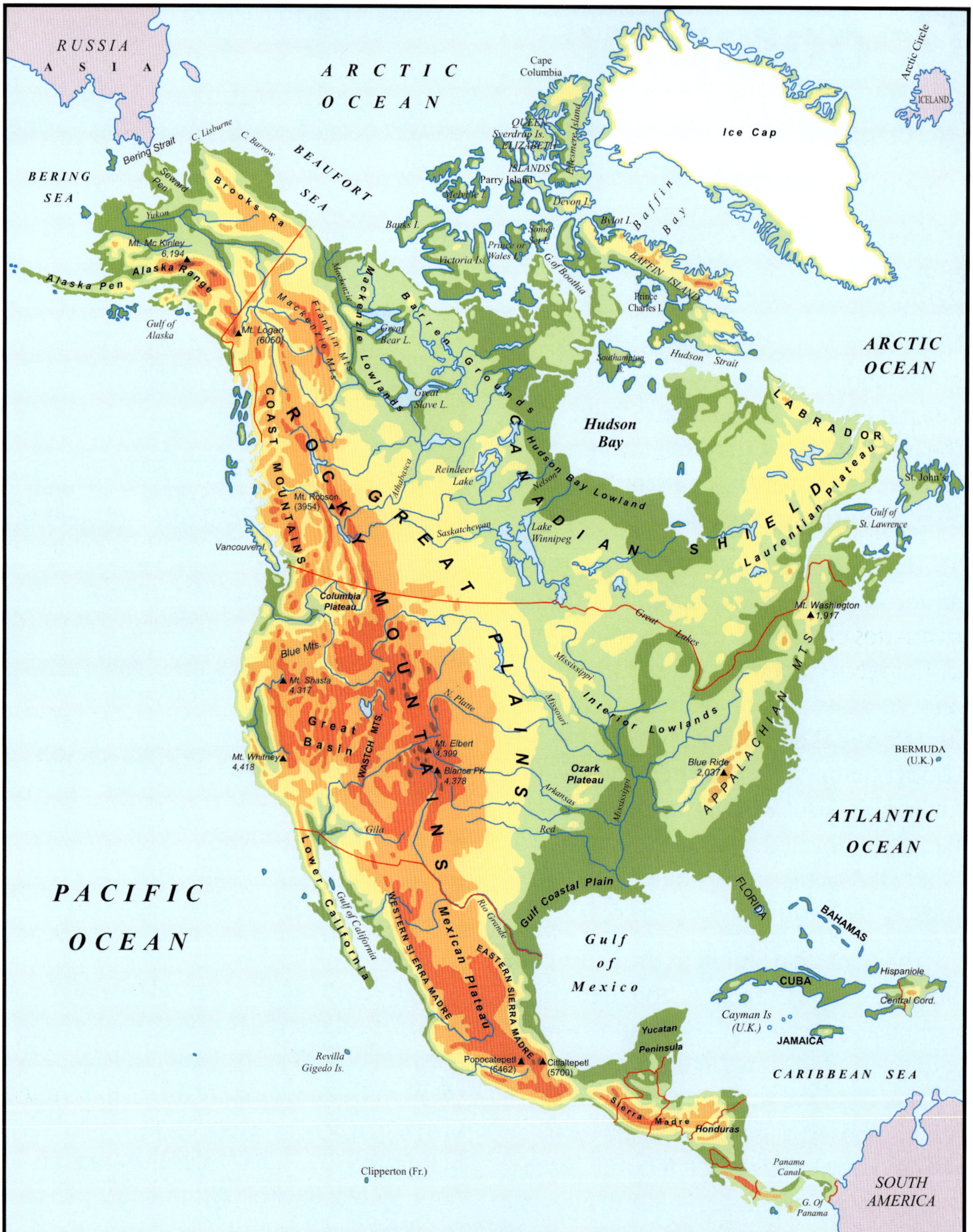
RUSSIA
A S I A
ARCTIC OCEAN
Cape Columbia
ICELAND
Arctic Circle
Ice Cap
QUEEN ELIZABETH ISLANDS
Sverdrup Is.
Ellesmere Island
Parry Island
Melville I.
Devon I.
Bering Strait
C. Lisburne
C. Barrow
BEAUFORT SEA
BERING SEA
Seward Pen
Brooks Ra
Yukon
Banks I.
Bylot I.
Baffin Bay
Somerset I.
Prince of Wales I.
Victoria Is.
G. of Boothia
BAFFIN ISLAND
Mt. Mc Kinley 6,194
Alaska Range
Alaska Pen
Mackenzie
Mackenzie Mts
Franklin Mts.
Mackenzie Lowlands
Great Bear L.
Barren Grounds
Prince Charles I.
Gulf of Alaska
Mt. Logan (6050)
ARCTIC OCEAN
Southampton I.
Hudson Strait
Great Slave L.
Hudson Bay
LABRADOR
COAST MOUNTAINS
ROCKY MOUNTAINS
GREAT PLAINS
CANADIAN SHIELD
Athabasca
Reindeer Lake
Nelson
Hudson Bay Lowland
Laurentian Plateau
St. John's
Mt. Robson (3954)
Saskatchewan
Lake Winnipeg
Gulf of St. Lawrence
Vancouver I.
Columbia Plateau
Great Lakes
Mt. Washington 1,917
Blue Mts.
Mississippi
Mt. Shasta 4,317
N. Platte
Missouri
Interior Lowlands
APPALACHIAN MTS
Great Basin
WASTCH MTS.
Mt. Elbert 4,399
Mt. Whitney 4,418
Blanca PK 4,378
Ozark Plateau
Blue Ride 2,037
BERMUDA (U.K.)
Arkansas
ATLANTIC OCEAN
Gila
Red
Lower California
PACIFIC OCEAN
Gulf of California
WESTERN SIERRA MADRE
Mexican Plateau
Rio Grande
Gulf Coastal Plain
FLORIDA
BAHAMAS
EASTERN SIERRA MADRE
Gulf of Mexico
CUBA
Hispaniole
Central Cord.
Cayman Is (U.K.)
JAMAICA
Yucatan Peninsula
Revilla Gigedo Is.
Popocatepetl (5462)
Citlaltepetl (5700)
CARIBBEAN SEA
Sierra Madre
Honduras
Clipperton (Fr.)
Panama Canal
SOUTH AMERICA
G. Of Panama

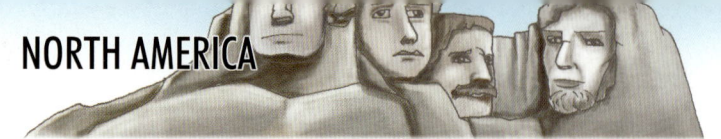

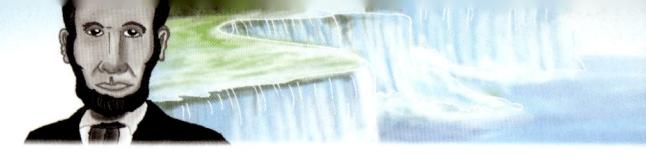

Geography

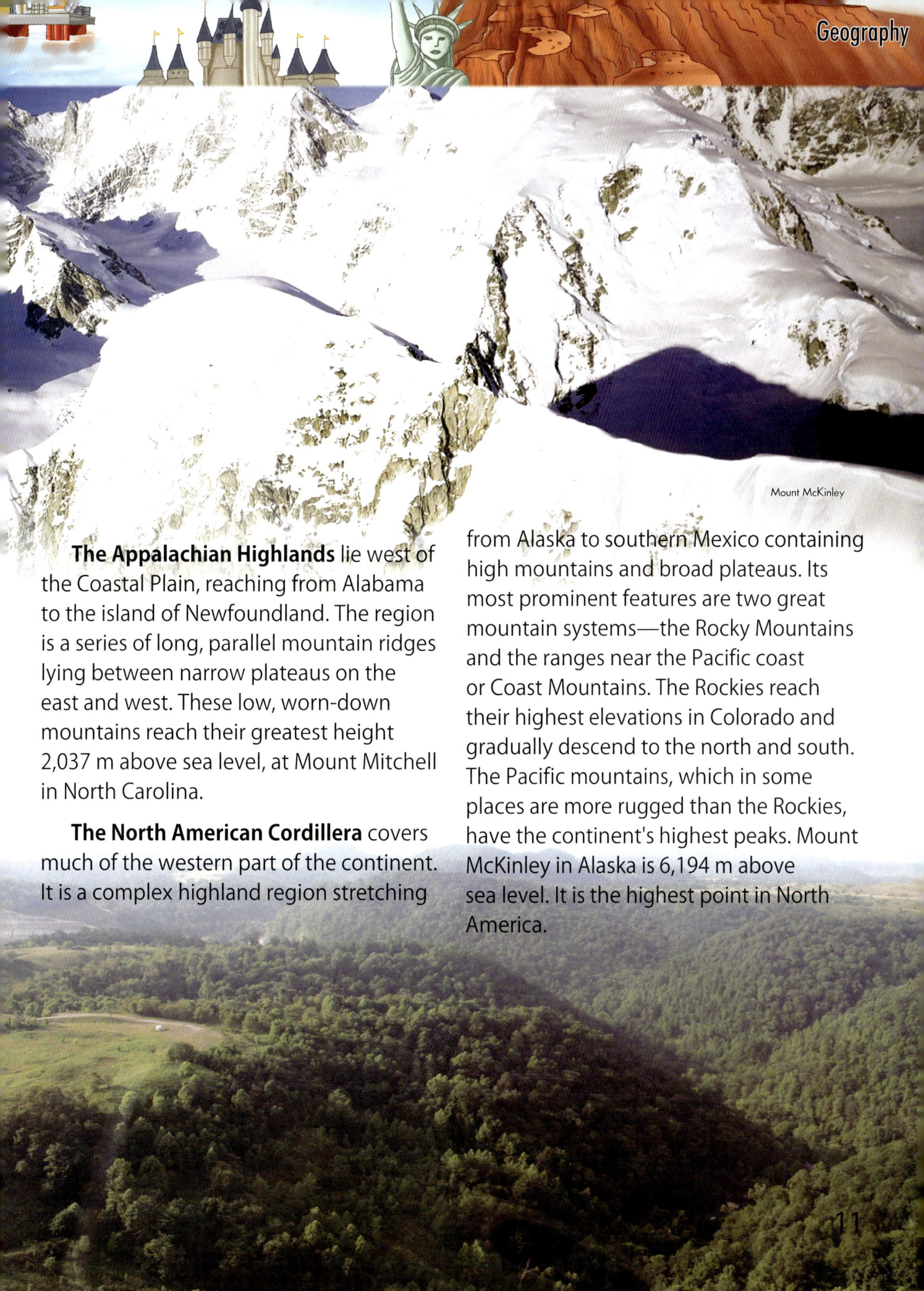

Mount McKinley

The Appalachian Highlands lie west of the Coastal Plain, reaching from Alabama to the island of Newfoundland. The region is a series of long, parallel mountain ridges lying between narrow plateaus on the east and west. These low, worn-down mountains reach their greatest height 2,037 m above sea level, at Mount Mitchell in North Carolina.

The North American Cordillera covers much of the western part of the continent. It is a complex highland region stretching from Alaska to southern Mexico containing high mountains and broad plateaus. Its most prominent features are two great mountain systems—the Rocky Mountains and the ranges near the Pacific coast or Coast Mountains. The Rockies reach their highest elevations in Colorado and gradually descend to the north and south. The Pacific mountains, which in some places are more rugged than the Rockies, have the continent's highest peaks. Mount McKinley in Alaska is 6,194 m above sea level. It is the highest point in North America.

NORTH AMERICA

Astonishing fact

The coastline of North America is the longest coastline of all continents.

Paricutin volcano

volcanic mountains south of Mexico City contains Mexico's highest peaks.

The Antillean System meets the North American Cordillera on the south, moves east and southeast from southern Mexico through Central America and the islands of the Antilles. The western peaks of Central America are normally the highest in the region and have active volcanoes.

The large size of the continent makes possible the existence of long rivers, and two of the longest rivers in the world, the Mississippi and Mackenzie rivers flow across the continent. Two of the Mississippi's tributaries, the Ohio and the Missouri are themselves major rivers.

Between these two mountain systems (Rockies and Coast Mountains) are plateaus, basins and scattered mountain ranges. This pattern continues southward, where Mexico's Central Plateau is bordered by the Sierra Madres on the east and west. A belt of

Natural resources

North America is extremely rich in minerals. Almost all of the important minerals are found in large quantities in North America. However, the deposits of tin, manganese, chromium and diamonds are scarce.

Natural gas is primarily found in the south-central United States, especially Texas, Louisiana and Oklahoma. Major oil fields are located along the Gulf of Mexico in both Mexico and the United States and in California, Alaska and the Prairie Provinces of Canada. Coal is also produced in large quantities mainly in the eastern half of the United States.

A large variety of metals are also mined in North America, including almost half of the world's uranium and more than a quarter of the world's silver, copper, nickel, zinc and lead. North America also produces significant amounts of iron ore, gold and bauxite. Most of these metals are produced in United States and Canada and Jamaica. Mexico is also a significant producer of most of these metals and is a leading producer of silver.

Oil rig

> **North America produces a third of the world's total output of natural gas and about a fifth of the world's total output of coal and petroleum.**

NORTH AMERICA

Climate

North America has a wide range of climates. About one-third of the continent, mainly in the southwest, has a dry climate. The Great Plains fall under the semi-arid climate receiving little rainfall.

The Arctic zone includes the Canadian Shield and Alaska and is dominated by polar climates; only in the months from June–September do the temperatures rise above the freezing point.

The cool temperate zone stretches south of the Canadian Shield from Newfoundland to Alaska and is dominated by the polar climate with long, severe winters.

The warm temperate zone covers the Mississippi lowlands and the south-eastern USA and is dominated by the tropical air coming from the Gulf. Winters are mild and the frost-free season lasts over six months. The south-western USA experiences a Mediterranean-type of climate, with dry summers and mild winters.

In coastal areas, especially the Pacific coast of Canada and the United States, variations in the season are less noticeable because of the moderating effect of the sea. Winds moving over the relatively warm ocean waters bring mild temperatures and moderate to heavy rain.

As one moves inwards, towards the south-western United States and northern Mexico, there is a decrease in rain and an increase in the temperatures, creating desert and near-desert conditions.

Temperate zones are those climate zones which do not have extreme summers or extreme winters. These regions are often found behind high mountains which restrict winds carrying moisture from reaching the other side of the mountains.

History

According to evidence found by archaeologists, human settlement in North America began 100,000 to 40,000 years ago, when Mongoloid people from Asia migrated over the Bering land bridge and east of the Brooks Range in Alaska into the heart of the continent. These people gave birth to empires and rich cultures, like the **Mayans** and **Aztecs**. They lived on the continent long before the arrival of the Europeans.

Aztecs

The first-known European settlement in North America was by Vikings in what they called Vinland. But permanent settlement came only after Christopher Columbus's voyage to the West Indies in 1492. As a result of the discovery of the New World, America provided new grounds for the establishment of colonies of European countries.

Aztec temple

NORTH AMERICA

In 1521 the Spanish destroyed the Aztec empire and imposed their rule on Mexico. The Spanish also colonized Central America and parts of what is now the southern USA, but most of the present USA and Canada was claimed and explored by traders and colonizers from the Netherlands, France, and England. Britain and France contested for territory in North America and the Caribbean.

The early European settlers of North America revolted against the colonial rule in 1776 in the great American Revolution which eventually led to their freedom from the colonial rule. The American Revolution had a great impact across the continent. Most importantly it directly led to the creation of the United States of America.

Mexico and Central America won their independence from Spain in 1821. The USA reached its present continental extent by acquiring its southwest region in 1848 and 1851 as a result of war with Mexico, and by purchasing Alaska from Russia in 1867.

A Canadian confederation with continuing links to Great Britain was formed in 1867 north of the USA.

Religion

The large majority of North Americans are Christians. The majority of the English-speaking Christians in North America are Protestant, but certain national groups such as those of Irish, Polish and Italian descent are predominantly Roman Catholic and those from the Balkan countries are largely Eastern Orthodox. The Jewish population of North America is concentrated in the large cities. Generally, the Spanish and French speaking people are members of the Roman Catholic Church.

Some Americans of Asian origins have stuck to their religions. There are mostly Buddhists in the group followed by Confucians. There are also many Muslims and Hindus. Almost every religion found in Europe and Asia is present in North America.

Basilica of the National Shrine of the Immaculate Conception

Although many Native Indians are Christians, some have retained their traditional religions which are basically forms of nature worship. **Shamanism** is prevalent among the Inuit (Eskimos). **Voodoo** is practiced in Haiti and by some Gulf Coast black people. Santeria, a mixture of African religious beliefs and Roman Catholicism, is practiced in parts of Cuba and by some Cubans living in the United States.

Touro Synagogue
Newport, Rhode Island

NORTH AMERICA

Festivals

The word 'epiphany' comes from the Greek word epiphaneia which means manifestation.

Epiphany

Epiphany

The festival of Epiphany falls on the 12th day after Christmas. It marks the manifestation of Jesus Christ to the three Magi, the baptism of Jesus, and the miracle of the wine at the marriage feast at Cana. It is one of the three major Christian festivals along with Christmas and Easter. Epiphany originally marked the beginning of the carnival season preceding Lent, and the evening before it is known as Twelfth Night.

Mardi Gras

Mardi Gras or Shrove Tuesday falls on the day before Ash Wednesday and marks the end of the carnival season, which began on the day of Epiphany. Celebrations are held in several American cities, particularly New Orleans.

Mardi Gras

Festivals

Ash Wednesday

Ash Wednesday

Ash Wednesday is the first day of Lent. It is a day of public penance and is marked in the Roman Catholic Church by the burning of the palms blessed on the previous year's Palm Sunday. The priest marks a cross with his thumb with the ashes from the palms upon the forehead of each worshipper. The Anglican Church and a few Protestant groups in the United States also observe the day but generally without the use of ashes.

Passover

The Feast of the Passover also known as the Feast of Unleavened Bread, marks the escape of the Jews from Egypt as described in the bible. As the Jews fled from Egypt, they ate unleavened bread. Since then during Passover, bread is replaced by **matzoh** (brittle flat bread eaten at Passover) in Jewish houses.

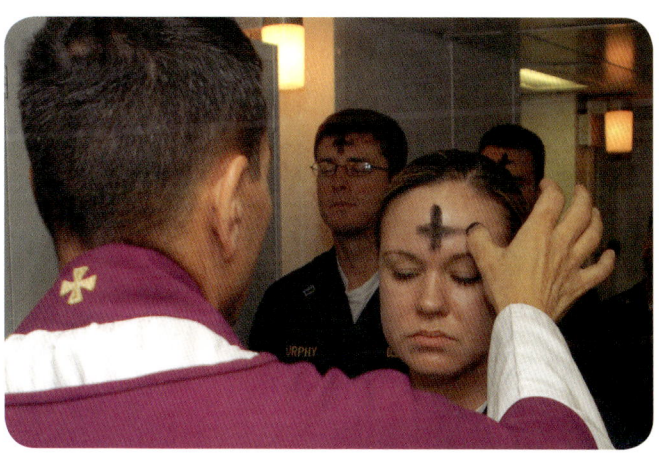
Ash Wednesday

The feast of Passover

NORTH AMERICA

Pentecost

Good Friday

Good Friday is the Friday before Easter. The day marks the Crucifixion, which is retold during services from the Gospel according to St. John.

Easter

Observed in all Western Christian churches, Easter marks the Resurrection of Jesus. It is celebrated on the first Sunday after the full moon that occurs on March 21 and is therefore celebrated between March 22 and April 25.

May Day

Although celebrated with far greater fanfare in other countries, May Day in the United States is a celebration of spring as well as a day honouring organized labour.

Pentecost

This day commemorates the descent of the Holy Ghost upon the apostles 50 days after the Resurrection. It is also known as 'Whitsunday' and is believed to have come from 'white Sunday,' when, among the English, white robes were worn by those baptized on the day.

May Day

Festivals

Independence Day

The Independence Day is the day of the adoption of the Declaration of Independence in 1776, celebrated in all the states and territories of United States of America. The day was first celebrated in 1777 in Philadelphia.

Halloween

Halloween

Eve of All Saints' Day, formerly called All Hallows and Hallow mass, Halloween is traditionally associated in some countries with customs such as bonfires, masquerading and the telling of ghost stories. These are old Celtic practices marking the beginning of winter.

Thanksgiving

Thanksgiving is the day of thanking god for good harvest. The festival was brought to the continent by the early European settlers. It is a federal holiday observed on the fourth Thursday in November by act of Congress (1941). It was the first such national proclamation issued by President Lincoln in 1863.

Hanukkah (Festival of Lights)

This festival was started in 165 B.C. to celebrate the purification of the Temple of Jerusalem. The festival lasts for eight days and in Jewish homes a lamp or candle is lighted on each night of the festival.

Christmas (Feast of the Nativity)

The most widely celebrated holiday of the Christian year, Christmas is observed as the anniversary of the birth of Jesus. On this day people decorate their Christmas trees and give presents to each other. The festival is a great favourite among children as they wait for Santa Claus who brings gifts and candies for them.

Christmas

NORTH AMERICA

Famous places

Statue of Liberty

The **Statue of Liberty Enlightening the World** was a gift of friendship from the people of France to the people of the United States. The Statue of Liberty was dedicated to the spirit of freedom by the French to the Americans on October 28, 1886.

The idea of the statue was proposed by the French historian Edouard de Laboulaye to mark the alliance between France and America during the American Revolution. The statue was designed by French sculptor Frederic-Auguste Bartholdi. Its framework of gigantic steel supports was designed by Eugene-Emmanuel Viollet-le-Duc and Alexandre-Gustave Eiffel, the latter famous for his design of the Eiffel Tower in Paris.

Niagara Falls

The **Niagara Falls** is a voluminous waterfall on the Niagara River, straddling the international border between the Canadian province of Ontario and the U.S. state of New York. The falls are 27 km north-northwest of Buffalo, New York and 121 km south-southeast of Toronto, Ontario.

Niagara Falls is divided into the Horseshoe Falls and the American Falls. The Horseshoe Falls drop about 53 m and the height of the American Falls varies between 21–30 m because of the presence of giant boulders at its base. The larger Horseshoe Falls are about 790 m wide, while the American Falls are 320 m wide.

Niagara Falls

Famous places

American Museum of Natural History

American Museum of Natural History

The **American Museum of Natural History** located on the Upper West Side of Manhattan in New York City, is one of the largest and most celebrated museums in the world. Located in park-like grounds across the street from Central Park, the Museum comprises 25 interconnected buildings that house 46 permanent exhibition halls, research laboratories and its renowned library. The collections contain over 32 million specimens, of which only a small fraction can be displayed at any given time.

Grand Canyon

Grand Canyon, the great gorge of the Colorado River is one of the natural wonders of the world. The multicoloured rocks and other eroded rock forms catch the contrast of sun and shadow and glow with changing hues of great beauty.

The first European to see the canyon was the Spanish explorer Garcia Lopez de Cárdenas in 1540. The Grand Canyon was declared by the U.S. government in 1908 as a national monument.

Grand Canyon

NORTH AMERICA

Death Valley

Death Valley

Death Valley National Park, established on February 11, 1933, covers almost 3,000 square miles and is a vast natural museum, larger than the Yellowstone National Park. The floor of the Valley is almost 300 ft below sea level (at Badwater basin) and it is recognized as the lowest point in the Western Hemisphere and one of the hottest places on Earth. 134 degrees F was recorded in 1913, second only to the 136 degrees registered in Libya in 1936.

Disney World

Disney World is a recreational resort owned by the Walt Disney Company's Walt Disney Parks and Resorts segment. The resort is located southwest of Orlando, Florida in the United States. With four theme parks, two water parks, 23 themed hotels to its credit, Walt Disney World Resort is one of the largest and most visited recreational resort in the world.

The history of Walt Disney World is quite fascinating. The resort opened on October 1, 1971, with just the Magic Kingdom theme park to its credit, and the admission cost of only $3.50 for an adult. The opening day itself saw a crowd of around 10,000 guests. More than a decade later, on October 1, 1982, Epcot, a theme park dedicated to international culture and technological innovation was added to the resort. May 1, 1989, saw the emergence of Disney's Hollywood Studios, while Disney's Animal Kingdom was added to the famed resort on April 22, 1998.

Disney World

Famous places

Mount Rushmore

Mount Rushmore, a United States landmark, is located in the Black Hills of South Dakota. Mount Rushmore, named in 1885 after a New York lawyer Charles E. Rushmore, was decided to be the spot for immortalization of U.S. history by Doane Robinson.

Robinson wanted a sculpture that acted as a 'gateway to the west'. He was not the first American who wanted to create a monument in the west. Missouri Senator Thomas Hart Benton wanted to make a memorial of Christopher Columbus in the Rocky Mountains. In the early 1920's Gutzon Borglum was carving a Confederate memorial on Stone Mountain in Georgia. He became the perfect person to create such an incredible wonder in South Dakota. The actual creation of this monument took six and half years.

Facts and figures about Mt. Rushmore

Sculptor	John Gutzon de la Mothe Borglum
Presidents depicted	George Washington, Thomas Jefferson, Theodore 'Teddy' Roosevelt and Abraham Lincoln
Height of the faces	60 ft from chin to forehead (as tall as a 6-floor building)
Elevation of Mt. Rushmore	5,725 ft
Dates of Construction	From 1927 to 1941
Location	The Black Hills of South Dakota (near Keystone SD)

NORTH AMERICA

Galapagos Islands

The Galapagos Islands are an archipelago composed by five major islands located very near the equatorial line to 972 km west of continental territory of Ecuador in the Pacific Ocean. They are considered a true natural wonder of the World. The main Islands of the archipelago are Isabella, Fernandina, San Cristobal, San Salvador and Santa Cruz. In addition to the five major islands, there are also 8 other large islands and around forty islets and smaller rocks. The capital of the province is Puerto Baquerizo Moreno, a small city located in the San Cristobal Island. The total area of the islands is around 8000 square km.

The Galapagos Islands hosts some of the most impressive wildlife of the world; but, not only because flora and fauna of the islands is so beautiful; but, also because they have evolved without human presence, therefore they are virtually fearless of human presence.

The famous scientist Charles Darwin, who laid down the Theory of Evolution, visited the islands in September 1835. The Galapagos are today most closely associated with Darwin. He made extensive collections of the plants and animals and was struck by the fact that closely related species were found on different islands.

After many years of research and thought he published **The Origin of Species** in 1859, which put forward the concept of evolution by natural selection. In later life, Darwin maintained that the Galapagos were the source of all his ideas and research.

Galapagos Island

Famous places

The Bay of Fundy

The Bay of Fundy is renowned for having the highest tides on the planet (16.2 m). One hundred billion tons of sea water flow in and out of the Bay of Fundy twice daily. Fundy's extreme tides create a dynamic and diverse marine ecosystem. The Bay is renowned for its coastal rock formations, extreme tidal effects (vertical, horizontal, rapids and bores) and sustainable coastal development. It is also a critical international feeding ground for migratory birds, a vibrant habitat for rare and endangered Right whales, and one of the world's most significant plant and animal fossil discovery regions. The Bay of Fundy is located between the Canadian provinces of New Brunswick and Nova Scotia on North America's east coast.

Tikal Mayan Ruins

Tikal, pronounced, 'teeKhal' is the second largest of the ancient ruined cities of the Mayan world civilization, second only to **Calakmul**, the largest ancient Mayan city. Located in El Petén, Guatemala, where regions are distinguished by departments rather than states, **Tikal** has recently become one of Guatemla's most sought after tourist destination. Near the cities of Flores and Santa Elena Tikal is also one of the best preserved Mayan archaeological sites in South America alongside **Chichen Itza** and **Machu Pichu**.

The Maya city of Tikal

27

Famous people

George Washington

George Washington (1732-1799) was the first President of the United States of America. He served as President from April 30, 1789, until March 4, 1797 (two terms). His Vice-President was John Adams (1735-1826), who was later voted the second President of USA. George Washington became known as 'The Father of Our Country'.

George Washington

Abraham Lincoln

Abraham Lincoln (February 12, 1809- April 15th, 1865) was the 16th President of the United States of America. He served as the President from March 4, 1861, until April 15, 1865 (he was re-elected in 1864). Lincoln's Vice-President was Andrew Johnson (1808-1875).

Lincoln was elected President in 1860. During Lincoln's presidency, the Southern states withdrew from the Union because Lincoln and the Northern states were against slavery. Six weeks after becoming President, the Civil War began. In this war, the Northern states (which stayed in the Union) fought the Southern states (called the Confederacy). The Civil War lasted from 1861 until 1865.

On January 1, 1863, Lincoln issued the Emancipation Proclamation, which eventually led to the freeing of all slaves in the USA. During the Civil War, Lincoln gave many speeches, including the Gettysburg Address (November, 1863), a short speech in which he stated how a country must be dedicated to human freedom in order to survive.

On April 14, 1865 President Lincoln and Mrs. Lincoln were attending a play at Ford's Theatre in Washington D.C. While there, he was assassinated by John Wilkes Booth, an actor with extremist views concerning politics and slavery. There had been a conspiracy by Booth and his cohorts to not only kill the president, but also William Henry Seward, Secretary of State in Lincoln's Cabinet, and Andrew Johnson, the vice-president. The attack on Seward failed and the one on Johnson was never carried out. The president, after being shot, was carried to a house across the street from the theatre and he died nine hours later. Booth was killed by one of the men trying to seize him.

Abraham Lincoln

Famous people

Muhammad Ali

Muhammad Ali

Muhammad Ali AKA Cassius Clay is a world famous heavyweight boxer. He won the World Heavyweight Championships 3 times. He also has an Olympic Gold medal. After winning the amateur 'Golden Gloves' championship in 1959 and 1960, Cassius Clay became Olympic light-heavyweight champion in 1960. He immediately became a professional and within four years he was the heavyweight champion of the world.

Walt Disney

Walter was an American film producer, director, screenwriter, voice actor, animator, entrepreneur and entertainer, who created Mickey Mouse in 1928 and Donald Duck in 1934. These quickly became the world's favourite cartoon characters. He then started making full-length animated films, including Snow White and the Seven Dwarfs (1937), Pinocchio (1940) and Bambi (1942). Sometimes he was criticized for changing famous stories to suit his cartoons.

His film company became the biggest producer of cartoons, but it also made children's films with real actors such as '20,000 Leagues under the Sea' (1954) and films such as 'Mary Poppins' (1964) which combined cartoon characters and real actors. Disney is now one of the most successful film companies in the world, making films for adults as well as children. In 1954 Walt Disney opened Disneyland, the huge amusement park in California.

Walt Disney

NORTH AMERICA

Tiger Woods

Tiger Woods is one of the best golfers to have ever lived. He is supposedly the first billionaire pursing a sports career. He has 14 Major wins. He was also the youngest and first of any African descent to win The Master gold Tournament.

Michael Jeffery Jordan

Michael Jordan

Michael Jeffery Jordan is sometimes considered the greatest basketball player ever. He won the NBA championships 6 times. He was a seasonal Most Valued Player 5 times, Finals Most Valued Player 6 times, All-Star Most Valued Player 3 times and has been placed in the Basketball Hall of Fame.

Jordan is renowned in professional American basketball for his high scoring. By 1992 he had achieved a record average of 32.3 points in 589 games for the Bulls. He is known as 'Air' Jordan because of the height he can leap!

Tiger Woods

Famous people

Muhammad Ali

Muhammad Ali

Muhammad Ali AKA Cassius Clay is a world famous heavyweight boxer. He won the World Heavyweight Championships 3 times. He also has an Olympic Gold medal. After winning the amateur 'Golden Gloves' championship in 1959 and 1960, Cassius Clay became Olympic light-heavyweight champion in 1960. He immediately became a professional and within four years he was the heavyweight champion of the world.

Walt Disney

Walter was an American film producer, director, screenwriter, voice actor, animator, entrepreneur and entertainer, who created Mickey Mouse in 1928 and Donald Duck in 1934. These quickly became the world's favourite cartoon characters. He then started making full-length animated films, including Snow White and the Seven Dwarfs (1937), Pinocchio (1940) and Bambi (1942). Sometimes he was criticized for changing famous stories to suit his cartoons.

His film company became the biggest producer of cartoons, but it also made children's films with real actors such as '20,000 Leagues under the Sea' (1954) and films such as 'Mary Poppins' (1964) which combined cartoon characters and real actors. Disney is now one of the most successful film companies in the world, making films for adults as well as children. In 1954 Walt Disney opened Disneyland, the huge amusement park in California.

Walt Disney

NORTH AMERICA

Tiger Woods

Tiger Woods is one of the best golfers to have ever lived. He is supposedly the first billionaire pursing a sports career. He has 14 Major wins. He was also the youngest and first of any African descent to win The Master gold Tournament.

Michael Jeffery Jordan

Michael Jordan

Michael Jeffery Jordan is sometimes considered the greatest basketball player ever. He won the NBA championships 6 times. He was a seasonal Most Valued Player 5 times, Finals Most Valued Player 6 times, All-Star Most Valued Player 3 times and has been placed in the Basketball Hall of Fame.

Jordan is renowned in professional American basketball for his high scoring. By 1992 he had achieved a record average of 32.3 points in 589 games for the Bulls. He is known as 'Air' Jordan because of the height he can leap!

Tiger Woods

Test Your MEMORY

1. Name the only strip of land connecting North America to South America.
2. Name the three major countries which occupy most of the land space of North America.
3. Who was the first European to suggest that the Americas were not a part of Asia as Christopher Columbus had suggested?
4. Name the northernmost point on the mainland.
5. When is the festival of Epiphany celebrated?
6. When is the Independence Day of America celebrated?
7. Who gifted the Statue of Liberty to the people of America?
8. What is the name of the sculptor of Mt. Rushmore?
9. Name the Presidents depicted on the Mount Rushmore.
10. Who was the first President of the United States of America?
11. Who was Abraham Lincoln?
12. Who created the world famous cartoon characters of Mickey Mouse and Donald Duck?

NORTH AMERICA

Index

A
Aleuts 6
American Museum of Natural History 23
American Revolution 16, 22
Anglo-America 5
Antillean System 9, 12
Appalachian Highlands 9, 10, 11
archaeologists 15
Arctic Circle 3
Ash Wednesday 18, 19
Aztecs 15

C
Canadian Shield 9, 14
Central America 3, 5, 12, 16
Charles Darwin 26
Charles E. Rushmore 25
Christians 17
Christmas 18, 21
Coastal Plains 9

D
Death Valley 6, 24
Disney World 24

E
Easter 18, 20
Eiffel Tower 22
Epiphany 18
European Union 3

G
Galapagos Islands 26
Good Friday 20

Grand Canyon 23
Gulf of Mexico 3, 13

H
Halloween 21
Hanukkah 21
hemisphere 3, 24

I
Independence Day 21
Interior Plains 9, 10
Inuit 6, 17
Isthmus 3, 9

J
Jesus Christ 18
Jewish 17, 19, 21

L
Latin America 5, 6
Lent 18, 19

M
Mackenzie 12
Mardi gras 18
matzoh 19
Maya 6
Mayans 15, 27
May Day 20
McKinley 6, 11
Mexico 3, 5, 8, 9, 11, 12, 13, 14, 16
Mississippi 9, 12, 14
Missouri 12, 25
Mongoloid 15
Mount Rushmore 25

N
New World 4, 15
Niagara Falls 22
North American Cordillera 9, 11, 12

O
Ohio 12
orthodox 17

P
Passover 19
Pentecost 20
plain 9, 11
polar 14
Protestant 17, 19

R
Roman Catholic 17, 19

S
semi-arid 14
slaves 4, 29
Statue of Liberty 22

T
temperate 14
Thanksgiving 21
Tikal 27
Tropic of Cancer 3

V
Vikings 15

---

* Maps not to scale; for illustration purpose only.